Musicdotes

for _Marty._
May they add
the extra seasoning
to the wonderful
World of music.
Have fun!

Gabriele

December 15, 1977

MUSICDOTES is published by
Ten Speed Press, 900 Modoc, Berkeley, California 94707

Library of Congress Cataloging in Publication Data:

Beach, Scott, 1931—
    Musicdotes.

    1. Music—Anecdotes, facetiae, satire, etc.
I. Title.
ML65.B42   780   76-30883
ISBN 0-913668-64-8

Printed in the United States of America

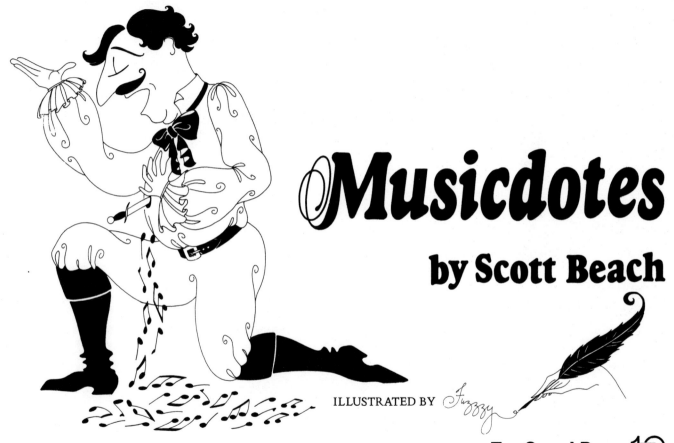

Musicdotes

by Scott Beach

ILLUSTRATED BY *Fuzzy*

Ten Speed Press 1⊕

To my loving friends and friendly lovers.

ON**ext** time you hear Chopin's "Mazurka in G-Major" (Op. 67, #1), listen carefully to the main theme. It's a bunch of freckles. Chopin had a long and torrid affair with George Sand.* She had freckles. All over. During an afternoon of dalliance, Chopin became fascinated with those dots, blots, and splotches. He drew a five-line staff and a treble clef on one of Sand's dunes. (I'll bet it tickled.) Letting the freckles fall where they may, he copied the resulting notes and used them for the main theme of his mazurka. George Sand's freckles are thus forever enshrined in Chopin's Opus 67, #1.

If you tell that story to someone else, you may wish to add that it isn't true. I made it up. I don't even know if George Sand *had* any freckles. The reason for this fabrication is to show that a story need not be historically accurate to be good.

Many of the stories in this book are old chestnuts, retold here just because they're good stories. Some, though I can't offer much proof, are, most likely, folklore. They're included because they're a charming part of our heritage. I make no apology for any of these tales that may be exposed as false. I'm not a historian. I'm a story-teller.

---

* Pseudonym of the Baronne Dudevant.

(The truth about that Chopin mazurka may be stranger than fiction. According to *Grove's Dictionary of Music and Musicians*, Chopin dedicated it to Mademoiselle Mlokosiewiczówna. That just *has* to mean something!)

In some cases, I've found more than one version of a story. The championship goes to the tale of the cop who tells the offstage trumpeter, "You can't blow that thing here! There's a concert going on!" I've heard or read variations of that story in connection with Leopold Stokowski, Edwin Franko Goldman, Artur Rodzinski, Vladimir Golschmann, and Arthur Fiedler. It wouldn't surprise me if it were told of every band and orchestra that ever played the *Leonore* Overture outdoors since Beethoven composed it.

The way these things work, I'm confident that my story about George Sand's freckles will one day be recited as gospel. All it wants is for a few people to pass it along. Of course, if it's repeated in print, it will then have the cachet of respectability and authority. Permission is hereby given.

I don't claim to have included all the best anecdotes about music and musicians. Many people will know other stories or other versions which properly belong in such a collection. This is just a sampling of my favorites. I'll follow up with something like "Son of Musicdotes" some other time. That time will come all the sooner if readers who share my passion for these stories send me their favorites that don't appear in these pages.

✶ ✶ ✶

I owe thanks and recognition to several people for their help in the preparation of this book. "Musicdotes" began as a feature on station KKHI, San Francisco. Len Mattson, the station's perennially elfin sales-manager, first suggested the idea, and much of the blame is his.

Jerome Fried, editor, agent, master trivialist, guided my every step and gave lavishly of his fabulous store of knowledge and skill. In Jerry Fried, the noble traditions of John Kieran and Franklin P. Adams are living still. By rights, he should be declared a national park.

Neva Beach listened and read and commented and counseled. Her sense of the appropriate is abundant.

Many of these stories have come from listeners and from music buffs of my acquaintance. I thank them all.

CONTENTS

Conductors

When I was five, my mother got me scrubbed, dressed, and briefed for my first symphony concert. She told me about the pieces we'd hear and cautioned me to avoid fidgeting during the program. I went along, full of excited anticipation.

To my young eyes, the Portland Civic Auditorium was the biggest room in the world. We had good seats on the main floor, and as I looked around and up into the balconies people by the zillions were filling the rows . . . more people than I'd seen in one place before, even at the Rose Festival Parade.

On the stage, people in important black clothes came out carrying instruments. They tuned and noodled, all facing a small platform at the center. A sense of excitement and anticipation swelled with the welter of notes and sounds. I broke my mother's commandment and fidgeted.

Presently, the house lights dimmed and the noodling and tuning stopped. The huge hall fell silent. It was the kind of silence that makes your hair stand up. Then — he came!

A man with a lot of flowing white hair strode onto the stage, and the room erupted at once with applause. He carried a thin white stick. He bowed, the godly creature, and then he turned off the applause by the simple trick of turning around and raising the stick. All eyes were on that white wand. The world held its breath. The stick moved. Music came!

I was awe-struck. If the stick moved faster, so did the music. If it made tiny motions, the music got tiny. And when the stick made a gigantic smashing gesture, like a magic pencil drawing an explosion, there was a gigantic smashing explosion in the music! At the end of each piece, the conductor bowed as the audience applauded enthusiastically. Small wonder! The man was obviously a great magician.

Back at home, I remembered little of the music we'd heard. But that white stick stayed in my mind, dancing, wiggling, sweeping, and swooping, making music happen. I got one of my mother's knitting needles and gave it a try. I waved the needle, expecting the house to be engulfed in sound. No music came, nothing but a whoosh as the needle split the air.

3

One of my grandmothers, a Christian Science practitioner, explained that it was a matter of faith. If I had faith enough, the music would come. She gave faith a boost by starting the phonograph, and I began a distinguished career as conductor of our Victrola.

Now, though I've attended countless symphony concerts, operas, band recitals, and musical shows, and though I've played in orchestras and even done a bit of conducting, the image of that thin white stick as a magic wand is still vivid. Part of me will always believe that the conductor makes the music with the baton.

Many orchestra musicians probably suspect, sadly, that all conductors share that belief.

Allegro Perduto

When Antal Dorati was in charge of the Minneapolis Symphony, I met one of the players who told me to "Watch him when he conducts and when he starts making a circular scooping motion with his arms, that will mean, 'Keep playing, boys, I'll find my place.'"

Applausible Story

At the end of a concert by the Boston Symphony conducted by Sir Thomas Beecham, the audience broke into a wild ovation, bringing Sir Thomas back for numerous bows. He soon grew tired of the ritual and held up his hand. "Ladies and gentlemen, when I was a very young conductor, I heard a deaf vicar in the front row say to his neighbor, 'Why is he bowing? The musicians did all the work.' So I shall now leave, and you may applaud these gentlemen to your hearts' content."

Figure 19

Another example of Sir Thomas Beecham's flair for elegant language: He once stopped a rehearsal to address the cymbalist. "At figure 19, a grand smash of your delightful instruments to help in the general welter of sound, if you please."

Più

In 1910, at Covent Garden, Sir Thomas Beecham was conducting the opening night of Strauss' *Elektra*. Apparently, Sir Thomas was not much impressed with the abilities of the members of the cast. He began urging the orchestra to play more and more forte. "The singers think they're going to be heard, and I'm going to make jolly well certain that they are not."

Tempo Tantrum

Arturo Toscanini was once given a fine gold watch by the members of his orchestra. He carried it proudly. Once, during a rehearsal, Toscanini substituted a cheap drugstore watch, and when the orchestra made some goofs he whipped out the watch and stomped it to smithereens. Thinking it was the presentation watch, the orchestra reacted in mild shock, and when they continued the rehearsal there were no more goofs.

Finale

Gaetano Merola, the much revered general director of the San Francisco Opera, died while conducting a pops concert in San Francisco's Stern Grove in 1953. The program included "Un bel di . . ." from *Madama Butterfly*.

The aria contains the words: "Io, senza dar risposta me ne starò nascosta un pò per celia, e un pò per non morire al primo incontro." (I, without answering, will stay hidden partly for fun, and partly so as not to die at the first meeting.)

As the soprano sang those words, Merola's arm stopped, just before a downbeat. He froze, his eyes stared blankly, and then he fell from the podium to the floor. The word at which Merola expired was "morire" (to die).

An old Italian tradition holds that a man should not die with his feet on the ground. Merola's final action was to fall so that his feet stayed up on the podium.

6

A Different Drummer

Pierre Monteux was rehearsing the San Francisco Symphony in *Wellington's Victory*, Beethoven's spectacular evocation of the Battle of Vittoria. On the stage, two batteries of percussion were situated on either side, representing the guns of the French and English armies. The bass drum of the French contingent got lost and began firing salvos not in the score. Monteux stopped. "Monsieur, you cannot change history! It is written that the English will win this battle. So just play what is printed."

Egalité

Pierre Monteux was once on tour and was dismayed to learn that a certain hotel had overlooked his reservation. The hotel manager was quite cool until he learned that Monteux was a great and celebrated conductor. He blurted, "I didn't realize that you are *somebody*. Of course I will give you a room." Monteux said, "Monsieur, everybody is somebody."

Pop-Up

Boris Sirpo was conducting a performance of Strauss' "Death and Transfiguration." A long-held dominant chord resolves to its tonic at a climactic point. Giving the cue for this dramatic moment, Sirpo hit his music stand with the baton, and three inches of the end snapped off and flew straight up in the air. As though he did this every day of his life, Sirpo, still conducting, stuck out his left hand and caught the flying baton-tip, precisely on the third beat of the measure. He finished the piece with a self-satisfied smile.

Detour

George Frideric Handel was conducting a concert one evening, with the celebrated violinist Matthew Dubourg as soloist. Dubourg missed a cue and got completely lost . . . he hesitated and began improvising, searching his mind for the correct key and phrase. At last, he got back on the track, and Handel cracked up both the orchestra and the audience, saying, "Welcome home, Mr. Dubourg."

Who Indeed?

The story is told . . . and I seriously doubt it really happened . . . of a symphony conductor who was rather more ambitious than gifted. During a rehearsal, this ill-fated stick-waver so upset the seasoned professionals in the orchestra that the tympanist gave one of his kettledrums an exasperated, noisy swat and threw the stick over his shoulder. The conductor stopped, on hearing this unscheduled explosion, and demanded, "Who did that?"

You Can Tell the Players Without a Score

At least one fellow-conductor did not join in the general admiration of Arturo Toscanini's storied memory. Hans Knappertsbusch preferred to have the score before him at all times. When someone remarked on this deviation from the current rage, Knappertsbusch was unmoved. "Yes, I use the score. And why not? *I* can read music."

N.B. This story has been told of a number of conductors who also use the score while conducting. The most recent notable citation is that of Sir Georg Solti.

The practice of conducting without the score is fairly modern. Once, when Leopold Stokowski performed one of these feats of memory, an old lady in the audience remarked, "But isn't it a shame that that nice Mr. Stokowski can't read music? Imagine what a great musician he could be if he only knew how!"

"You should not perspire when conducting: only the audience should get warm."

— Richard Strauss

Hmm?

Fritz Reiner was conducting a rehearsal of a Wagner opera at the San Francisco Opera. The bass clarinetist, having many long rests to count, was in the habit of letting his head nod forward, listening with just enough attention to be ready to sit up and play the next cue. Reiner noticed this apparent somnolence and stopped to demand, "Mr. Fragali, do you know where we are?" The answer was immediate: "No, Maestro. I'm lost, too."

Pregnant Pause

During a two-week period, Leopold Stokowski instructed the Philadelphia Orchestra's librarian to keep a certain work handy for rehearsing. The score included a part which played only at the beginning and end, with some 500 bars of rest between cues. The musician who would play that part was about to become a father. He had a perfect record of attendance at rehearsals and performances. When the word came from the nearby hospital that the birth was expected momentarily, Stokowski called for the score. The musician played his first cue, calmly set down his instrument, and left the hall, counting measures. He went to the hospital, still counting, saw his new baby, kissed his wife, and got back in his chair at the Academy of Music in time to play the finale, his record intact. Stokowski is reported to have smiled with more-than-usual warmth.

10

Peek-a-boo-boo

Fritz Reiner had a distinctly delicate conducting style. His gestures were usually quite small and reserved. The story is told of one player whose eyesight was rather weak. In desperation to see the maestro's beat, he came to a rehearsal with a brass telescope, which he proceeded to set up, trained on the podium. What he saw when he got the focus was Reiner glowering at him and saying, "You're fired!"

440 or Fight

During a symphony rehearsal, the cello section kept sounding out of tune. In exasperation, the conductor ordered the rehearsal stopped while the cellists were sent, one by one, to his dressing room where he would tune each one personally. The players lined up in the hallway. As each musician came out, he passed the same cello to the next, so that the maestro retuned the same instrument about a dozen times. When the session was over, the rehearsal was resumed, and the conductor was quite satisfied with the sound of the cello section.

He Missed a Chance to Shut Up

Serge Koussevitzky went to the bedside of a Boston Symphony musician who was near to dying. The musician took this terminal opportunity to read Koussevitzky off for being a tyrant, selfish, cruel, and heartless. The maestro did his best to tell the expiring second violinist that he thought of his players as his beloved children. The player recovered from his illness . . . and though he lived and played for several more years, Koussevitzky never forgave him.

Troppo Subito

Leopold Stokowski used to love to take his orchestra by surprise. He'd come on stage for a rehearsal, leap to the podium, demand "Strauss, letter F!" and instantly begin gesturing. This usually caught most of the players unprepared. Stokowski would display great impatience and grandly take it again. On one such occasion, when only a few players managed to find and play their notes, Stokowski barked, "Too late!" One unruffled player stood and said, "Too soon!" Stokowski smiled a rare smile and went on with the rehearsal.

Fee, Fie

Because of his deep respect . . . near unto veneration . . . for the works of Verdi, Toscanini once accepted an invitation to conduct at a Verdi festival on the condition that he be paid no money at all. Another conductor, jealous of Toscanini's renown, didn't know of these arrangements. He haughtily demanded to be paid one lira more than whatever Toscanini got. The management complied to the letter and gave the poor fellow a check for one lira.

Virtu-oh-so!

Shortly after Serge Koussevitzky took over the Boston Symphony, the orchestra's bass section asked him to play for them. Koussevitzky was a noted virtuoso of that ponderous instrument. He consented, and the musicale was attended by many members of the symphony, including a cellist who later said, "It was astounding! I never heard such bass playing. I closed my eyes and said to myself. 'That is not a bass. It sounds like a lousy cello!'"

Out of the mouths . . .

Orchestra musicians often dislike having a conductor lecture them on phrasing and other basic matters. An oboist in a celebrated orchestra once interrupted the maestro's oration to say, "Oh, any fool can see that!" The conductor smiled a Cheshire cat smile: "I'll have to take *your* word for that, sir."

Trade Secret

Bruno Walter told of an orchestra musician who finally realized his dream of conducting. After his first podium experience, he talked with the legendary conductor Hans Richter, who asked how it went. "Oh, it went very well," said the fledgling. "You know, Maestro, this business of conducting is really very simple." Richter put a finger to his lips: "Shh! I beg you, don't give us away."

It's the Legs that Go First

Serge Koussevitzky stopped a rehearsal of the Boston Symphony to chide a player, saying, "Don't play like an old man." The player came back with "You're an old man yourself." The Maestro was unruffled. "I know that. But when I conduct like an old man, I will give up the job." The rehearsal resumed and the musician gave it his best.

Downbeat

Sir Thomas Beecham got held up in traffic one night and arrived at the Covent Garden Opera House only moments before the performance was to begin. A stand-in was all ready to enter the pit when Beecham puffed into view, flung his coat and hat aside, and made his way to the podium. He received the warm applause of the audience, turned, raised his baton, and asked the concert-master, "By the way, what opera are we doing tonight?" "It's *La Bohème*, Sir Thomas." "Ah, to be sure," said Beecham, and gave a lordly downbeat.

Caution:
Conducting can be dangerous to your health.

Not long ago we heard of a conductor who got too involved in his work and stabbed himself in the hand with his baton. The great French composer J.B. Lully used to conduct in the old style of pounding out the rhythm on the floor with a large cane or staff. One night he brought the cane down on his foot ... and the foot developed gangrene ... and he died of it.

Oops!

During a rehearsal of Tchaikovsky's "Romeo and Juliet Overture-Fantasia," the conductor was unsatisfied with the attack on the kettledrums at a place where a large explosion is called for. He kept saying, "A little more, please." The tympanist finally gave it all he had, and the stick went right through the drumhead with a sickening rip. The conductor stopped and said, "A little less, please."

If at first you don't succeed...

From time to time, Toscanini would lose his temper during a rehearsal and snap his baton into little pieces. He once blew up because of a particularly bad bit of playing and tried to break his baton. It was made of extremely limber wood, and it wouldn't break. In his frustration, Toscanini turned his wrath on a handkerchief from his pocket. It wouldn't tear. At last, the furious maestro took off his coat and ripped it to shreds. Only then did he take a breath and announce, "We shall take it again."

In the Grand Manure

Here's another of those stories which may or may not be true ... but it's just too good a story to quibble over accuracy. Sir Thomas Beecham was conducting a performance of *Aïda* in a small English town. The production was something less than superb. A horse on the stage suddenly began adding to the decoration of the set. Beecham spoke to his players in hushed tones, "Upon my word, gentlemen, he's a critic."

15

16

Sir Thomas Requests the Pleasure

Few conductors have ever matched the urbane wit and pointed sarcasms of Sir Thomas Beecham. During a rehearsal, when a player lost his place, producing a number of false notes, Beecham stopped and said, "We do not expect you to follow us all the time, but if you would have the goodness to keep in touch with us occasionally . . ."

Louder, Please

Sir Thomas was conducting a rehearsal of a work which called for some mighty big sounds in the brass. Beecham wasn't satisfied by the playing of a trombone. He addressed this question to the player: "Are you producing as much sound as possible from that quaint and antique drainage system which you are applying to your face?" Sir Thomas took it again and got his fortissimo.

Threat

I don't know if this is a true story, but it's a good one. There was a conductor who tried, not very successfully, to cover a degree of ineptness with displays of temperament. Once, in New York, he berated a musician during a rehearsal, saying the playing was all wrong. The musician stopped the diatribe and broke up the rehearsal by saying, "Look, buddy, if you keep on like that I'm going to follow your beat."

Words and Music

Louis Antoine Jullien was a flamboyant and showy conductor who specialized in grandiose productions that more resembled Busby Berkeley movies than symphony concerts. Near the end of his life, he seems to have gone off the trolley. He once undertook to set the Lord's Prayer to music. He never finished it, but remarked in a letter, "Think what a grand title page, 'The Lord's Prayer . . . words by Jesus Christ, music by Jullien.'"

In a Pinch

Christoph Willibald Gluck was a renowned composer and conductor. On the podium, he was a holy terror. During a rehearsal, Gluck was once angered by the inattention of a double bass player. He got down on hands and knees, crept up to the fellow, and gave him a healthy pinch on the posterior. The musician gave a whoop of surprised pain and fell to the floor, bass and all. After that, we assume, he paid attention to the conductor.

Good Old Costa

In the mid 1800s, England's most celebrated conductor was Michael Costa. He also tried his wings as a composer, though with very little success. In 1856, he composed an oratorio and sent the score to Rossini, along with a gift of Stilton cheese. Rossini commented, "Good old Costa has sent me an oratorio and some cheese. The cheese was very good."

Nuts!

Toscanini was famous for occasional eruptions of anger when a player fouled up a passage. Once, he upbraided an orchestra member whose playing he found inferior. The player fired back an insult and Toscanini ordered him off the stage. As he left, the player turned and shouted, "Nuts to you!" The maestro's retort was delivered fortissimo: "It is too late to apologize!"

Tell It Like It Is

The story is told of a conductor who stopped a rehearsal to rhapsodize: "The music should sound as if you were playing on top of a high mountain, overlooking a bank of clouds. You are fanned by the winds . . ."

"Look," said the concertmaster, "just tell us whether you want it played loud or soft."

De gustibus . . .

Arturo Toscanini, our era's maestro sine qua non, was known to be a devoted "ladies' man." He passionately enjoyed all the ceremonies of courtship and romantic celebration of womanly charm. Here's his own statement on the subject: "I kissed my first woman and smoked my first cigarette on the same day. I have never had time for tobacco since."

pppppp

A conductor was extremely fond of very soft sounds. During a rehearsal, he kept asking the French horns to play more softly . . . pianississimo. Finally, on a subtle cue from the first-chair player, the musicians held their horns at their lips but didn't play at all. The conductor was almost satisfied. "Splendid! Now just a wee bit softer and you'll have it!"

Barbed Remarks

In a rehearsal for *Messiah*, Sir Thomas Beecham said to the chorus, "When we sing 'All we, like sheep, have gone astray . . . ,' might we please have a little more regret and a little less satisfaction?" And when a soprano became upset and said, "Sir Thomas, I'll have you know that I am a lady!" Beecham smiled. "Madam, your secret is safe with me."

A Matter of Record

Arturo Toscanini once tuned in a radio broadcast of Beethoven's Seventh Symphony. As he listened, he muttered about poor phrasing, clumsy interpretation, bad playing. When the recorded performance was over, Toscanini launched into a diatribe about how the whole thing missed the mark and left Beethoven in the cold. By now, you've probably guessed it: the recording was conducted by Arturo Toscanini.

To the Finnish

Leopold Stokowski reigned for decades as one of the all-time super showmen of the podium. Conducting without a baton, using special spotlights to highlight his white hair or project the shadow of his hands on the ceiling, Stokowski electrified audiences and occasionally horrified purists. The Finnish composer Jean Sibelius said, "He is a very fine man, I am sure . . . a very interesting man, and interested in many things — but not, I think, in music."

. . . Carefully

The following dialogue took place between Sir Thomas Beecham and a tenor during rehearsals for *Die Meistersinger*.

Beecham:

   Have you ever made love?

Tenor:

   Yes, Sir Thomas.

Beecham:

   Do you consider yours a suitable way of making love to Eva?

Tenor:

   Well, there are different ways of making love.

Beecham:

   Observing your grave, deliberate ways of making love, I was reminded of that estimable quadruped, the hedgehog.

Notable Memory

There are many stories about Toscanini's phenomenal memory. One of them sounds a bit farfetched, but it could have happened. Just before a concert, a clarinetist came to Toscanini and said his E-natural key was broken, and he wouldn't play that night. The maestro shut his eyes for a moment and said, "It's all right; you don't have an E-natural tonight."

Follow the Leader

Leopold Stokowski hated to have people arrive late for symphony concerts. Once, to show the public how it feels, he had members of the orchestra straggle onstage, stand around, wander about the hall, and chat amiably with each other. The concertgoers, accustomed to a highly casual way of life, got the message, and at the next concert everybody was there a few minutes early, audience, players, Stokowski, and all.

22

Composers

Shameless Pun

Shortly after the death of Beethoven, a caretaker was tending the shrubbery near the great composer's tomb. He stopped in fright on hearing a sound from within the crypt, a faint musical sound . . . four notes repeated in the same pattern: a long note followed by three short ones a major third higher. The caretaker dropped his shears and ran to the superintendent's office. The police were summoned, along with a minister and a musical scholar. They hurried to the cemetery and stood with their ears against the stone. The same four notes came forth. At once, the scholar laughed aloud. "That's the Fifth Symphony theme, backwards. Beethoven is decomposing."

Button, Button

Charles Gounod's wife wanted to be sure her husband was well dressed for his public appearances. She presented him with a fine suit of formal clothes. The buttons on the coat and trousers were one-of-a-kind, cloisonné. Gounod was something of a philanderer, and during an afternoon with a certain countess one of those buttons popped off and fell to the parquet. The countess pounced on the button and took it to her jeweler to have a locket made. The prize was enshrined in the locket. Some time later, the countess had tea with Madame Gounod, who noticed the lovely locket and exclaimed, "How beautiful! May I see inside?" I don't have a punch line for this story, but you probably don't need one.

Dot's Dot

During a rehearsal for one of his compositions, so the story goes, Richard Strauss stopped and told a player, "No! No! That's a half-note! It isn't dotted." The player took a moment to look closely at the music on the stand. "Excuse me, Maestro . . . there's a fly-speck there . . . I thought it was a dot."

Strauss gave the cue to take it again . . . but stopped, thought for a moment, and said, "No . . . the fly was right."

Second Tenorio

Casanova learned that Mozart was composing an opera about Don Juan. He went to Wolfgang and regaled him with stories of his famous conquests, hoping, no doubt, to convince Mozart to change the story and make it about Casanova. Up to that time, Mozart had thought that Don Giovanni wasn't a very nice guy. But after hearing Casanova's litany, he went ahead and created a masterpiece . . . called *Don Giovanni*.

It's Easy if You Nose How

Mozart once wrote a piece for the harpsichord and told Haydn, "You'll never be able to play it." Haydn gave it a try, but stopped short when he came to a measure where a single note in the middle of the keyboard came on the same beat on which there were chords on the extreme high and low ends of the instrument. When Haydn said, "This is impossible," Mozart sat down and showed him how. He played the high chord with his right hand, the low one with his left, and the note in the middle with his nose. Haydn commented, "With your nose, it looks easy."

25

Haydn-Go-Seek

The Prince of Austria decided that Haydn's body should be dug up and reburied in a more honored place. When the simple casket was opened, it was discovered that the great composer had lost his head. Phrenology was all the rage at that time. That's the dubious science which studies bumps on the skull. And darned if some phrenologist hadn't made off with Haydn's noggin . . . said it had a very big "music-bump." And though it seems hard to believe, Haydn's head didn't get back to the rest of Haydn until 1954!

Igor Was Eager

This story probably didn't happen . . . but it's still a good yarn. George Gershwin wrote to Igor Stravinsky in Paris to ask how much he charged for lessons. Came back the question: "How much is your annual income?" Gershwin replied: "About $100,000." Stravinsky cabled back: "Am coming to America. How much do *you* charge for lessons?" It's so good a tale that it's also told of Gershwin and Ravel.

Can't Take It

George Antheil's *Ballet Mécanique* is scored, among other things, for car horns, fire siren, airplane propeller, ten grand pianos, six xylophones, and four bass drums. At a performance at Carnegie Hall, a man in the third row could take no more than eight minutes of the din. He tied his handkerchief to his cane and raised the white flag. The surrender brought down the house.

That's Up Near Buffalo, Ain't It?

The composer of *La Traviata, Rigoletto, Otello,* and so many other all-time operatic favorites started out by writing an opera that never got produced and has never been heard of since. Verdi's first opera was called *Rocester.* Later, for reasons nobody could understand, Verdi wrote an overture to *The Barber of Seville.* Then he got two arias into an opera called *Faust* and gave it up as a bad job. Of course, he did manage to scribble a few winners. But wouldn't you just love to see a production of Verdi's *Rochester*?

Young Master

The Archbishop of Salzburg just couldn't believe that the young Wolfgang Amadeus Mozart was all that prodigious. To prove that his billing was correct, Mozart confined himself in a room for ten days, seeing only a meal-servant, while he composed a mass. When the work was completed, the Archbishop was nice enough to say that the kid was pretty good, after all.

Dis-Krenek-ted

Samuel Goldwyn was planning a movie with a Czech setting. Ben Hecht and George Antheil approached the legendary mogul to urge him to hire Ernst Krenek to create the score. Krenek was in Hollywood at the time, and he needed money.

"Never heard of him. What has he written?"

Hecht and Antheil rattled off a list of Krenek's works, but Goldwyn had heard of none of them. Antheil embroidered the story, adding, "And he wrote *The Threepenny Opera*!"

Hecht joined in, "And *Rosenkavalier* . . . and *Faust*! And *La Traviata*!"

Goldwyn's face lit up. "So he wrote *La Traviata*, did he? Well, just bring him around so's I can get my hands on him! Why, his publishers almost ruined me with a lawsuit just because we used a few bars of that lousy opera! We had to retake half of the picture for a few lousy bars!"

Krenek didn't get the job.

Kate the Great

On the occasion of her coronation, Catherine the Great commissioned the composition of an opera. She wrote the libretto herself and called it *Minerva's Triumph*. The opera never did very well, possibly because it took two weeks to perform. Two other imperial flopskys followed before Catherine retired from the field. The first was *The Early Reign of Oleg, the Varangian*, and the second was *Buslaevich, the Novgorodian Hero*. Disastrovich!

Highest Bidder

Jacques Halévy became irritated when an organ grinder stood outside his window cranking out tunes from Rossini's *Barber of Seville*. He went outside and made an offer to the street musician. "I will pay you one louis d'or if you will stand outside Rossini's window and play one of my tunes."

The organ grinder smiled, "But Rossini paid me *two* louis d'or to play *his* music outside *your* window!"

Bologna

Gioacchino Rossini loved all kinds of hearty food. One of his favorite snacks was a fresh bologna sandwich. Rossini appears to have given one of the musicians in the opera orchestra the extra assignment of preparing this delicacy for his enjoyment during the first intermission. In a number of Rossini first acts, the second oboe plays only at the beginning and finale. The assumption is that, while everybody else was making music, the second oboe was making a bologna sandwich.

Sou Me!

A young performer got a small role in Offenbach's *Les Deux Aveugles.* The pay was a few francs a month. At the first rehearsal, Offenbach told the young man to cross the stage and throw a sou into a blind man's hat. "I'm sorry," said the fellow, "I can't take this role." "Why? Isn't it important enough?" "No, sir, it's because of the sou. You see, I haven't got one." "Oh," said Offenbach, and thereupon gave him a raise.

Diamonds Are Forever?

When Beethoven completed his monumental Ninth Symphony, he offered it, according to custom, to King Friedrich Wilhelm III of Prussia. His majesty was graciously pleased to send back a letter and a diamond ring. Beethoven needed money more than baubles ... a common complaint among composers ... and he dashed to a jeweler to sell the ring. The jeweler handed it back after one squint through his loupe. It was a fake.

. . . and a Partridge in a Pear Tree

In Mühlhausen, Johann Sebastian Bach got the job as organist at St. Blasius' Church. The contract called for Bach to be paid, annually, 85 gulden, 54 bushels of grain, 2 cords of wood, 2 dozen fish, threescore fagots for kindling, to be delivered to the door, in lieu of acreage. The contract was signed on June 15, 1707. Apparently, Bach didn't consider himself too well paid. After a little over a year, he quit to take another job that paid, presumably, more gulden, more grain, more fish, and more cordwood.

A Narrow Escape

In 1814, an invading army sacked the town of Roncole in Italy. Many of Roncole's women and children hid in the town's church. But the invaders broke in and spared no one. One mother escaped the carnage with her baby by climbing to the belfry. She stayed up there until the terror was passed. Generations of opera-lovers would have missed a lot if the baby had shared the fate of the others below. His name was Giuseppe Verdi.

The Proper Study

The Los Angeles Philharmonic scheduled an all-Villa-Lobos concert, to be conducted by the composer. Before Villa-Lobos arrived, the orchestra had been fully rehearsed, but he demanded two full sessions. The orchestra manager argued, "They don't need that much rehearsing. They already play your pieces perfectly." Villa-Lobos insisted. "But *I* have to rehearse so I can learn how to conduct my pieces!"

The Bald Impresarios

Gioacchino Rossini was never bothered by the pressures of his work. Deadlines frightened him not a bit. He once remarked to a friend, "The best time to compose an overture is the evening before opening night. Nothing primes inspiration more than necessity, whether it be the presence of a copyist waiting for your work or the prodding of an impresario tearing his hair. In my time, all the impresarios in Italy were bald at thirty."

Statuesque

When Rossini was seventy, some friends and admirers came to tell him they had raised 20,000 francs to erect a monument to their favorite composer. Rossini was moved by the tribute, but he had a constant need for ready cash. He said, "Give *me* the twenty thousand and *I'll* stand on the pedestal!"

Cross My Psalm with Silver

King Louis XII of France once promised the court composer Josquin des Prés a raise, and then proceeded to forget his promise. Des Prés was moved to compose a motet on a phrase from the 119th Psalm, "Oh, think upon Thy servant as concerning Thy word." The king heard the motet and got the message. The raise came through. Des Prés was so happy that he wrote another motet on another phrase from the same Psalm: "Oh, Lord, Thou hast dealt graciously with Thy servant."

31

Borrowing from Peter

In 1928, Richard Rodgers composed the score for "Chee-Chee," a musical based on Charles Petit's novel *The Son of the Grand Eunuch*. The story related the efforts of a young man to avoid being castrated. A bilateral orchitectomy[1] was a prerequisite for inheriting his father's exalted title.[2] At the point in the story where the hapless youngster is led off to be emasculated, Rodgers inserted

32

several bars from Tchaikowsky's *The Nutcracker*. In his autobiography, Rodgers says, "I found it gratifying that at almost every performance there were two or three individuals with ears musically sharp enough to appreciate the joke."

---

[1]You could look it up.
[2]In case you're wondering, the Grand Eunuch became a sire before he took office.

33

Ringing Performance

A starving musician once called on Gioacchino Rossini to ask for a handout. To earn the coins, he proceeded to play the "Prayer" from Rossini's *Moses* on glasses of water. During this ringing performance, a servant came in with an important message. Rossini told the servant to wait. "I'll be with you in a moment. This gentlemen is rinsing my prayer."

Allegro Confusione

A concert was once given in honor of Hector Berlioz. One of the finest of all concert violinists, Henri Wieniawski, played Berlioz' "Rêverie et Caprice." The number was very warmly received. Berlioz was delighted and said, "Never have I heard an artist who has so completely caught my meaning and has so wonderfully interpreted it." Wieniawski was, meanwhile, speaking to Felix Mendelssohn backstage. "I am glad I got through it. I never had such a task in my life. I have not the remotest idea what I have been playing or what the piece can be about."

Dvorsky?

If you know any of the piano compositions of Michel Dvorsky, then you also know as many works of Josef Hofmann. They were the same person. Hofmann was a celebrated concert pianist, and he also composed a lot of keyboard music. To avoid being accused of unreasonably favoring his own stuff, he signed several of his works "Michel Dvorsky." Hofmann's audiences apparently liked what they heard because the Dvorsky pieces were much requested. And it isn't bad business to be paying the royalties to yourself.

Off'n-beat

When Jacques Offenbach fired his valet, he made a point of giving him excellent references. Someone asked him why, if he had discharged the man, did he take such pains to help him find a good situation elsewhere? Offenbach explained that the poor fellow was a good valet, but he was no good for a composer. "He always beat my clothes outside my door . . . and the tempo was invariably wrong."

What Will We Name the Baby?

Of all the admirers of Richard Wagner, the conductor Hans von Bülow was surely the most ardent, not to mention broad-minded. While Von Bülow was conducting rehearsals for the première of *Tristan und Isolde*, Wagner was conducting an affair with Frau Cosima von Bülow. A baby girl was the issue of this ill-concealed dalliance. Far from playing the outraged husband, Von Bülow considered himself especially honored. Even went so far as to name the baby Isolde!

What'll He Do for an Encore?

One day, Louis XIV got extremely angry with his court musician, Jean Baptiste Lully, over some disagreement. At a performance that night, Lully tried everything he could to make his nibs happy again, even played his favorite piece as well as he could. Louis only glowered a royal glower. In desperation, Lully backed off to one side, got a good run, and landed, ker-smash, on the harpsichord, reducing it to rubbish. His Majesty was graciously pleased to smile, and all was forgiven.

Six Women, Five Men, and a Tenor

Gioacchino Rossini loved jokes. His final major work, the *Little Solemn Mass*, bears the composer's indication, ". . . for twelve singers of three sexes." Rossini composed an open letter to accompany the score: "Dear God, here it is, my poor little mass, done with a little skill, a bit of heart, and that's about all. Be Thou blessed, and admit me to Paradise."

Private Lesson

Pietro Mascagni was sitting in his study one day when a street musician stopped outside to play a Mascagni piece on his hand-crank barrel-organ. Mascagni listened for a while and then dashed outside, grabbed the crank, and played the piece at the proper tempo. Satisfied, the composer returned to his study. Next day, the street musician displayed a new sign that read, "Pupil of the celebrated Mascagni."

Aha!

Domenico Scarlatti kept a dog and a cat in his home. One afternoon, while the composer was working on a manuscript, the dog lit out after the cat. The cat executed an evasive maneuver, jump- ing smack onto the keyboard of Scarlatti's harpsi- chord. "Aha!" said the maestro. "You've found it!" He thereupon wrote one of his best-known pieces, "The Cat Fugue."

Hic Jacet

After Mozart died, his widow, Constanze, moved to Copenhagen, and later she married one G. N. Niessen, with whom she spent a few happy years before his death brought her widow's weeds out of the mothballs. Niessen was buried in fine style, with these words of tribute on his headstone: "Here rests Mozart's widow's second spouse." Sic transit gloria Niessen.

Takes All Kinds

Can you tell, only from hearing, whether a piano is being played by a man or a woman? Brahms claimed that he could, though he admitted that ". . . it is by no means an easy thing to distinguish, by the sense of hearing alone, a feminine man from a masculine woman."

Tacet

Hector Berlioz' teacher at the Paris Conservatory once asked, "Why do you include a two-measure rest in this passage?" Berlioz explained that he wanted an effect best produced by silence. "Good!" said the teacher, "Suppress the rest of the piece. The effect will be better still."

Eclat

George Frideric Handel wrote his *Royal Fireworks Music* for a big celebration staged by King George II to mark the signing of the Treaty of Aix-la-Chapelle. A tower was built to shoot the fireworks . . . and 101 cannon were lined up to add to the booms and bangs. When it came time for the show, a fire broke out and all the fireworks went off at once. Everybody ran for cover, and the *Royal Fireworks Music* didn't get played.

Kreisleriana

Fritz Kreisler was one of the most beloved musicians in history. He was especially admired for the delicacy and warmth of his tone. He had a practice of including in his violin recitals little-known works by great old masters: Vivaldi, Pugnani, Padre Martini, and others. In 1935, Kreisler finally confessed that many of those pieces were his own compositions written in the several styles of their supposed creators. He seemed to take special pleasure in having those works warmly received by audiences who thought they came from someone else.

... who help themselves

George Frideric Handel was not above grabbing another composer's ideas. In fact, musical historians have sleuthed out some truly blatant Handelian plagiarisms. But Handel was unabashed, even when caught redhanded. Once, when he was confronted for having lifted an entire aria for one of his operas, he declared, "Yes, but it was much too good for him."

Ursa Major

How's this for a description? "He was called 'The Great Bear' . . . for he was like a giant . . . broad, fat, thick, with large hands and feet, huge arms and thighs. His hands were so fat that the bones were lost in the flesh and formed dimples. His long face resembled that of a horse . . . later in life

a steer . . . and was drowned in fat, with double cheeks, three-fold chin, a broad, large straight nose, and red, off-standing ears. But when he smiled, it was the sun emerging from a dark cloud." That vivid description was written by Romain Rolland, and he was talking a about the composer of *Messiah*, George Frideric Handel.

Alias

The première of Berlioz' opera *Benvenuto Cellini* was a resounding flop. To salvage something from his hard work, Berlioz put together some of the orchestral pieces from the score and called it "Concert Overture for Benvenuto Cellini." At the first performance, the audience hissed and booed. On a hunch, Berlioz crossed out the title and gave the piece a new name: "Roman Carnival Overture." And voilà! A hit!

Not THE Guidon Saltanovich?

Nicholas Rimsky-Korsakov wrote fifteen operas, most of which are little remembered. One of them has the distinction of bearing one of the longest

titles in history: "The Tale of the Tsar Saltan, His Son, the Famous and Mighty Prince Guidon Saltanovich, and the Beautiful Swan Princess." Only one tune from this long-handled opera has survived, a short piece in the third act. We know it as "The Flight of the Bumblebee."

Defenestration

During a rehearsal of one of his operas, George Frideric Handel had a stormy disagreement with the leading soprano. In a rage, Handel grabbed her and hoisted her over a window ledge. Dangling in midair, the prima donna decided the maestro was right after all. Handel put her back on the floor and said, "I know you are a witch . . . but I am the devil himself."

Rimsky

The "Rimsky" in Rimsky-Korsakov was added by the composer's great-grandfather. The old man, an admiral, was something of a snob. To set himself apart from all the common Korsakovs, he tacked on Rimsky to the family name. "Rimsky" means

"Roman." The admiral had spent some time in Rome, and he chose to be called "Roman-Korsakov." Nicholas is darned lucky that the old man didn't spend his time in, say, New York. Who could take seriously a composer named Nicholas New Yorksky-Korsakov?

Poor Little Lambs

Pierre Ducré's "Chorus of Shepherds" was enthusiastically received by the critics when Hector Berlioz conducted its première. Berlioz announced that he had found the work on a closet shelf. When the reviews came out, full of praise for the Ducré piece, Berlioz laughed long and hard. He was accustomed to being chewed up by the critics. The "Chorus of Shepherds" was really Berlioz' own work, given the alias to fool his tormentors. Later, he expanded the composition and released it as "L'Enfance du Christ."

Ms. Mozart

When Mozart first met Marie Antoinette, he proposed marriage. She turned him down . . . by the way, they were both seven years old at the time. At twenty, Wolfgang fell in love again, but the lady married somebody else. To improve the odds, he moved in with her three sisters . . . the whole kaboodle. He finally chose Constanze to be his wife. She lived a long time, and was a good wife and a thoughtful widow.

41

Be My Guest!

George Frideric Handel was preparing his opera *Flavio Olobrio*. The tenor didn't like the maestro's accompaniment of his main aria. He shouted, "If you don't follow me better, I'll jump on your harpsichord and smash it to bits!" Handel replied, "Go right ahead . . . only please let me know when you do it so I can advertise. I'm sure more people will come to see you jump than hear you sing."

I Can Handel It

Having completed a section of his *Messiah*, George Frideric Handel sent for a singer to read it through. The singer made numerous mistakes. Handel was furious. "You scoundrel! Didn't you tell me you could sing at sight?"

"Yes, sir, I did. And I can; but not at *first* sight."

'J Ever Have One of Those Days

Ludwig van Beethoven was a great composer, but as a conductor he was a bad insurance risk. Once when he was conducting one of his piano concertos* from the piano, he jumped up to cue an orchestra passage and upset the candlesticks with his arm. The audience laughed, which made Beethoven angry. He summoned two boys to hold the candlesticks behind him as he took it again from the top. At the same place in the music, he again jumped up, and this time his gesture caught one of the boys in the breadbasket. The boy let out a yip and dropped the candlestick. The audience cracked up and Ludwig got so angry he banged both hands down on the keys so hard that six strings broke. It is not recorded if he ever finished the concert.

— What are Brahms?
— They're like Keats, only louder

Johannes Brahms was playing the piano one day while a friend played the cello. They decided to read through a cello sonata by Beethoven. After a

---

*I know the plural of "concerto" is "concerti." Care for some fried potati?

while, Brahms was playing nothing softer than forte, and a lot of it came out fortissimo. The cellist had to raise his voice to say, "Please! I can't hear my cello!" Brahms kept hammering away. "You're lucky! I can!"

En Garde

When George Frideric Handel was playing the harpsichord during a performance of Mattheson's *Cleopatra* at the Hamburg Opera House, Mattheson took exception to Handel's tempo and tried to shove him bodily off the bench. Handel succeeded in keeping his place, but there was bad blood. After the performance the two men stepped outside to have a duel. Handel missed Mattheson, and Mattheson hit Handel, right smack on a large waistcoat button which deflected the blade. If it hadn't we'd never have had a "Halleluiah Chorus." Handel, by the way, composed forty-two operas and thirteen pasticcios. A pasticcio is pretty easy to compose, since you use other people's music and a dab of your own.

And/Or

Richard Wagner's last words have impressed scholars, poets, and philosophers. With his dying breath, Wagner sighed, "die Heure! die Heure!" (The time! The time!) Many profound meanings have been read into that deathbed cry. But the truth may be more practical than profound. Wagner suffered a fatal heart attack while visiting his housemaid in her room for no light motive whatever. When the seizure hit him, he asked to be carried to his own room to keep his wife from knowing where he had been. Sinking back on his pillow, he said, "die Uhr! die Uhr!" He'd left his watch on the maid's bedside table.

Barrel House

A visitor to Giuseppe Verdi's vacation home in Italy was startled to see the place cluttered with a large number of barrel organs. Verdi was then at the peak of his fame. He explained that all these instruments were set to crank out tunes from his operas. The only way he could have a peaceful vacation was to hire all the barrel organs in town.

44

Moonlight Sonata

You can take your pick of stories about the inspiration for Beethoven's "Moonlight Sonata." In one version, we find the composer walking down the street and hearing someone playing his music on a piano. He goes into the humble apartment and discovers a young blind woman at the keyboard. He asks if he may play for her. She listens and knows at once that her visitor must be Beethoven himself. Beethoven is so moved that he then and there improvises the famous sonata while her heart fills with ineradicable joy. Seems pretty unlikely.

Another story is more believable. Beethoven had a pupil, the Countess Giulietta Guicciardi, with whom he had extra-musical relations. It was quite natural that he would dedicate the "Moonlight Sonata" to Giulietta. She preferred evening lessons.

Next!

The première performance of Rossini's *Barber of Seville* was a major disaster. A rival composer, Paisiello, had friends in the house to stage noisy demonstrations during the performance. Almaviva broke a guitar string . . . Don Basilio tripped on his costume . . . another singer fell through a trapdoor . . . and somebody let loose a cat on the stage. Pandemonium! The next performances went better, though . . . and Rossini was given a torchlight parade.

Opritchnik

Tchaikowsky had a tough time getting started as an opera composer. He made six attempts before actually finishing one and seeing it produced. It was titled *The Opritchnik*, and it was about the secret police under Ivan the Terrible. The opera was well received, but it lacked staying power. Later on, stories about secret police weren't so popular in Russia.

This England

Frédéric Chopin was touring in England and wrote to a friend of his experiences. "I have not yet played to any Englishwoman without her saying to me, 'Like water!'" Apparently, Chopin was unimpressed with the playing of the local pianists. "They all look at their hands, and play the wrong notes with much feeling." He summed up his feelings about the English: "Every creature here seems to have a screw loose! . . . Eccentric people, God help them!"

Prolific

Jacques Offenbach composed a handful of hits and a truckload of losers. In the first column, there's *Les Contes d'Hoffman*, *La Belle Hélène*, *Gaieté Parisienne*, and *La Grand-Duchesse de Gérolstein*. He wrote 103 operettas, most of which have stayed on the shelf since they were first performed. By the way, don't listen to those who claim it was 104 operettas. Offenbach gave one of them two titles, *Le Soldat Magicien* and *Le Fifre Enchanté*. But even with two titles, it never got anywhere.

Seventh-Inning Stretch

"A fig for the irresistible urge!" Thus wrote a critic, a contemporary of George Frideric Handel. He was talking about the tradition of the audience standing for the "Halleluiah Chorus" during *Messiah*. The critic claimed that the only reason the people stood was that King George and his family got to the performance late . . . in fact, when it was all but over. As the chorus broke into "Halleluiah!" the royal family appeared in the regal box, and the audience just naturally sprang to its feet. The critic was obviously not a very effective debunker, since audiences still take a seventh-inning stretch for the "Halleluiah Chorus."

Fanny and Felix

When Queen Victoria had special praise for one of Felix Mendelssohn's "Songs Without Words," the composer was no doubt gratified and embarrassed. Fact is, he wasn't the composer. It was written by his sister, Fanny Hensel. She had told her brother that she wanted to be a composer, but he hit the ceiling and said she should forget such frippery and stick to her husband and children. As a compromise, he agreed to publish some of her songs under the name Felix Mendelssohn. Her Britannic Majesty was applauding the wrong person.

Performers

Franck Sinatra

Jean Le Franc was the principal violist of the Boston Symphony. He was single-minded about music, and paid no attention to anything other than his orchestra and its repertoire. Frank Sinatra was in the audience at a Sunday concert, and he went backstage after the program to be greeted by a number of the players. Someone said to Le Franc, "Do you know Frank Sinatra?" "Sure I know the Franck Sonata," was the reply. "But who is this?"

La Mobile Donna

One of the most successful opera singers of them all was the soprano Amelita Galli-Curci. And her success seems odd to us today, because the few recordings we have of her singing show that she often sang out of tune. One possibly apocryphal story has it that someone asked Signora Galli-Curci why she let herself stray from the pitch with such abandon. The diva replied, "Why should I learn to sing in tune when I have made millions singing out of it?"

Why Johnny Should Practice

In a voice class at the Conservatoire National de Paris, one of my fellow students was singing an aria when the teacher, Georges Jouatte, stopped her. He told her the tempo was all wrong, too varied for Mozart, and the phrasing sloppy.

Jouatte warmed to his subject. "Look, I know your kind. You're pushy, good-looking, and you do have a voice. With some good coaching, *if* you pay attention, you'll be successful. You'll get high fees for singing in opera houses all over the world.

"While you're up there on the stage," he continued in a steady crescendo, "getting cheers for your high F-sharps, down in the pit sits a violinist. His entire life has been devoted to his instrument. No normal childhood ... nothing but scales, études, constant, grinding repetition. He dreamed of a concert career ... but it wasn't to be. He wound up in the pit at the Opéra. He gives private lessons to help keep his family in their fifth-floor walk-up. He's a good player, able to read any score and adapt to the styles of different conductors. His pay is pathetically small, next to nothing.

Despite his great skill and artistry, despite all those years of practice, despite his mastery of one of the most exacting skills in the world, he makes peanuts, and he's never even seen by the audience! And he has to follow *you*!"

The student stood by the piano, trembling. Jouatte handed her a copy of the score. "Now, from the beginning, and please have the decency to sing it the way it's written."

For Whom the Chime Tolled

During a symphony concert in Seattle, the bass-trombone player had a long wait for his next entrance and dozed off in his chair. He was leaning back at the time, and, suddenly, he went clear over, chair, trombone and all, smack into the rack of tubular chimes just behind him. As in the "domino theory," the chimes tipped clamorously over, to be caught at the last second by the chime player and restored to their upright posture. The conductor stopped, gave a curt instruction, and began again at letter G . . . with a wide-awake bass trombonist waiting for his next entrance.

Tall Story

Luigi Lablache was an operatic basso in the 19th century. He was nearly seven feet tall, and his voice was said to be of equal size. A man once came to his door by mistake, looking for the celebrated midget, General Tom Thumb. Lablache towered over the caller and boomed, "I am Tom Thumb. When I am at home, I relax."

One-Man Heat Wave

Another all-time chestnut: When Jascha Heifetz was a young man, he played a recital at Carnegie Hall. In the audience were several eminent musicians. One, a celebrated violinist, turned to his friend, a renowned keyboard virtuoso, and said, "Isn't it terribly hot in here?" The reply was cool: "Not for pianists."

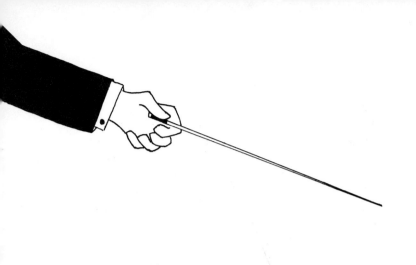

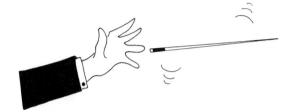

The Strange Case
of the Bassoon Player
and the Surgical Glove

I once knew a bassoon player who loved practical jokes. During a rehearsal, she stretched a surgical glove over the top end of her bassoon and stuffed the glove inside. Nothing happened until she played a low B-flat, which closes every hole on the instrument. The conductor froze in mid up-beat to see a hand suddenly pop out of the bassoon.

A Satisfied Man

The celebrated oboist Bruno Labate grew bored during a rehearsal when the conductor, Otto Klemperer, talked on and on about some fine points of intonation and phrasing. Labate interrupted the lecture, "Doctor Klemps, you talka too much." Someone later said to him, "I'd be scared to say a thing like that to Klemperer." Labate shrugged. "I got seventy-five thousand dollar in the bank. I no get scare."

Clavierst-hic

Josef Hofmann enjoyed retelling the story of a man who was refused admission to one of his recitals because he was drunk. The man bristled at the doorman and said, "Look here, you don't suppose I would go to a piano recital unless I *was* drunk?"

Noblesse Oblige

Emperor Francis the First of Austria was an amateur violinist . . . but not a very good one. Once he sat in as first fiddle in a string quartet rehearsal at the palace and ignored the flats in the key signature. The composer managed a masterpiece of diplomacy. "Would your Majesty grant my humble prayer for a most gracious B-flat?"

For My Next Selection . . .

Max Reger once played the piano in a performance of Schubert's "Trout Quintet." An admirer sent Reger a basket of trout as a tribute for fine playing. Reger was delighted, and for the next concert he pointedly announced that a minuet by Haydn would be featured. The title of the piece was significant: "The Minuet of the Ox."

Zara Zipper in the House?

The cellist Zara Nelsova gave a recital in Fargo, North Dakota. Following her last number, she stood carefully, bowed very tentatively, and walked sideways off the stage, clutching her cello. The zipper at the back of her gown had come unstuck, and Madame Nelsova was doing her best to avoid streaking her own concert.

Jascha or Mischa?

"To the greatest violinist in the world." An envelope bearing that inscription was brought to a table where Jascha Heifetz and Mischa Elman were dining. Both men looked at the envelope, and in mawkish deference each tried to pass it to the other. "You, Jascha." "No, you, Mischa." They agreed to open it together. Four of the world's most gifted hands unfolded the note. It began: "Dear Fritz."

(This story assumes that the reader knows that when Heifetz and Elman broke bread together, the other most celebrated violin virtuoso was Fritz Kreisler.)

Encore!

There's an old, old story of a singer who was giving a recital in Italy. After an aria, voices cried, "Bis! . . . Encore!" The singer obligingly repeated the number. Again, "Bis! Encore!" Just before he began a third such repetition, a voice shouted from the balcony, "You're going to keep singing it until you get it right!"

Next!

The composer Thomas Arne was asked to judge which of two singers was the better. Neither singer, unfortunately, was very good. After hearing their inept efforts, Arne said to one of them, 'You are the worst singer I have heard in my life." "Then I win!" said the other. "No!" said Arne, *"you* can't sing at all!"

Schlepp: To haul, drag, carry or otherwise schlepp

I was once on tour in a San Francisco Opera production of *Die Fledermaus*. One of the comprimario singers was Andrew Foldi in the role of the lawyer. We had dressing rooms on the third floor. When the stage manager called "places," Foldi went to the elevator, only to discover, when the doors slid open, that a few cans of garbage were being hauled out in the elevator. He drew back and let the doors close. In his richest basso, he said, "They can schlepp garbage — or they can schlepp Foldi — but garbage *and* Foldi, they can not schlepp!"

Bass Canard

Feodor Chaliapin was once on tour, thrilling audiences with his rich, Russian basso voice. He spent one of his free evenings with a young woman. In the morning, he told her, "I shall give you tickets for the opera this evening." The woman protested that she was poor, and in her hunger opera tickets were useless. "When one is hungry, one wants bread." Chaliapin's response was worthy of his reputation for the bon mot. "If you wanted bread, you should have spent the night with a baker."

56

I'll Wager

Niccolò Paganini was a superb violinist. As a gambler, though, he should have stuck to fiddling. Once, just before a concert, he got into a card game and did so badly that he lost all his money and ended by using his violin for a marker. The outlook for the concert was bleak until a sympathetic merchant loaned him a Guarnerius he happened to have around the house. Paganini played so brilliantly that the man said, "Keep the fiddle!" So the great virtuoso was lucky after all.

On another occasion, Paganini accepted a bet that he couldn't play a difficult concerto at sight without errors. Three movements later he had won the bet and collected a sure-enough Stradivarius! He never played it much, but it was a nice feeling to have a spare Strad.

The Ill-Tempered Clavierist

At the conclusion of a piano recital by Hans von Bülow, the audience gave him a resounding ovation. He played several encores, and it seemed that the people were ready to stay the night, listening and cheering. Von Bülow became impatient and signaled for silence. "If you don't stop this applause, I will play all of Bach's 48 preludes and fugues, from beginning to end!" That did it . . . everybody went home.

Hanging Together

A publication called *The Musical Standard* carried an unflattering review of a performance by one Henriette Sontag. The critic included this gem in his comments: "We hang on every note Madame Sontag sings — This proves the lady's great power of execution."

Eh?

A soprano whose sense of pitch was rather less than perfect was rehearsing with an orchestra for a concert. She kept landing either north or south of the notes in the score. The conductor, in some exasperation, finally turned and said: "Madam, I fear that we are not together. Will you please give the orchestra your A?"

PAGLIACCI!!!

No Hit

A newspaper in Arkansas was unimpressed with the talents of Enrico Caruso. The paper couldn't understand why a great pitcher like Walter Johnson could only get $600 a game while . . . and this is a verbatim quotation: ". . . Caruso, the Italian singer, gets about $3,000 a night for standing on the stage and screeching so no one but her own race knows what she says."

The Warsaw Kid

A New Orleans newspaper, *The Item*, had no available music critic to cover an appearance by Ignace Paderewski in 1896. The paper's boxing editor was sent to the recital hall. In his review, the scribe said: "In my opinion, he is the best two-handed piano fighter that ever wore hair." The review concluded with: "If I were a piano, I wouldn't travel as Paderewski's sparring partner for two-thirds of the gross receipts."

Grischa

Gregor Piatigorsky once confessed to a friend that he always felt nervous before a concert. The friend remarked that it was certainly not obvious. "When you come out on the stage, you seem to exude nothing but confidence."

Piatigorsky grinned. "I'm a good actor. Before a concert, I say to myself, 'Grischa, don't be nervous. You are the great Piatigorsky!'"

The friend asked, "And does it help?"

"No. I don't believe myself."

Where Is Beethoven?

Artur Schnabel was rehearsing a Beethoven piano concerto with Otto Klemperer on the podium. The two men disagreed as to the tempo of a certain passage, and Schnabel cavalierly began indicating his preference to the players behind the maestro's back. Klemperer saw this breach of etiquette and growled, "Herr Schnabel, the conductor is *here*!" Schnabel was unchagrined. "Ah . . . Klemperer is there and I am here . . . but *where* is Beethoven?"

Whew!

A sea captain once told me, in a salty growl, "The only people that whistle are damn fools and bos'n's mates." And whistling has been similarly unpopular on dry land, too. Ignace Paderewski, the great musician and statesman, put it this way: "Any man ought to have the right to shoot a whistler at sight."

"Too Loud, Mr. Green"

The noted symphonic bassist Jerry Green once recounted the following dream:

I was in Heaven, playing in the orchestra. It was a gigantic orchestra, with all the great players of history. Thousands of chairs! Paganini was the concertmaster. Heifetz was at the third desk, inside seat, in front of Ferdinand David. Virtuosi in every seat . . . Tartini, Glantz, Kincaid, Brain, Labate, Rubinstein, Primrose, Goodman. The harp section, of course, was enormous. But the bass section had only one player, me! God, Himself, was the conductor.

As we played our angelic music, the Maestro di

tutti maestri inspired us to fantastic heights. At one point, the music became so beautiful that the entire orchestra burst into holy flames! God stopped, tapped His baton, and the flames went out. He spoke to me. "Too loud, Mr. Green."

No, Thanks, I'll Stand

During an opera rehearsal, once, a technical problem kept the company standing around on the stage for a long time. One of the singers was Feodor Chaliapin, who began to display signs of impatience. An assistant rushed up to the great basso and asked if he wished to have a chair to sit on while the delay continued. Chaliapin replied, at about low B-flat, "My body is not weary. It is my soul that is weary. But my soul has no ass. So never mind the chair."

That's All

A musician in the Boston Symphony once told a fellow player that he was getting too old to keep up the pace of rehearsals and performances. He confided that he wanted to retire but was afraid to tell the conductor. The other smiled. "Just play for him."

That's Better; or, Let Your Fingers Do the Walking

The story is told of an extremely nervous and temperamental concert pianist who was about to begin a recital when he found that the piano bench was not at just the right height. He left the stage and came back with a telephone directory. He put the book on the bench and sat down. Not quite right, still. The pianist rose, opened the phone book, tore out a single page, and sat down again, happy with the whole thing, and played up a storm.

Cut-Rate

Fritz Kreisler was invited by a haughty society matron to play his violin at a soirée at her home. Kreisler set a fee of one thousand dollars. The grand dame agreed, but told him, "You will not mingle with my guests." Kreisler nodded. "In that case, my fee will be only five hundred dollars."

Little Corporal Punishment

Mstislav Rostropovitch owns and plays a Stradivari cello. There's a long scratch on one of the lower bouts. A previous owner of Rostropovitch's Strad once played before Napoleon Bonaparte. The Emperor said, "I've studied the cello. Let me try it out." He sat down and one of his spurs gouged that scratch in the wood. The damage has never been repaired. Who could resist being able to say, "That? Oh, Napoleon did it."

63

Opera

65

Count The Lines in This Story

If you set any store by numerology, consider Richard Wagner.

He was born in 1813. One, eight, one, and three add up to 13. There are 13 letters in the name Richard Wagner. He first performed in public in 1831, another year that adds up to 13.

His opera *Tännhauser* was completed on the 13th of April, 1844, and first performed in Paris on March 13, 1861. The first presentation of the Ring cycle began on August 13, 1876. Wagner spent some time as an exile in Saxony: 13 years. In all, he wrote 13 operas and died on February 13th in the 13th year of the new German Confederation.

Audience Participation

Richard Wagner's career as an opera composer got off to a rather shaky start. After composing two clinkers, full of impassioned scenes of romance and marriage, Wagner wrote another called *The Ban on Love (Das Liebesverbot)*. The opening (and, by the way, the closing) night of this number was a disaster. The orchestra became completely demoralized, singers kept forgetting their parts, and the husband of the prima donna took exception to the tenor's demeanor with his wife and bounded onto the stage to slug him in the face.

Exeunt Omnes

While he was still very young, Richard Wagner wrote a play. The plot was rather complicated. No fewer than forty characters got killed off by the end of Act II. In order to finish this hair-raising drama, Wagner had to bring some of the key people back as ghosts.

An Influential Critic?

When Verdi was putting finishing touches on *Il Trovatore*, an influential critic stopped by to hear the composer play some of the tunes. The critic was unequivocal: "Garbage! Rubbish! No good!" Far from being upset by the barrage, Verdi was delighted. "Thank you, my friend! I'm writing a popular opera. If I had pleased you, I should have pleased no one else. I'm most grateful for your opinion."

Kurt Remark

Before I appeared as Zuñiga in a recent San Francisco Spring Opera production of *Carmen*, I had to go through the interesting trial of an audition before the San Francisco Opera's redoubtable General Director, Kurt Herbert Adler. I sang a short Verdi aria while the maestro regarded me coolly from a wingback chair. After the last note, he glowered past braided fingers and finally said, in his charming Viennese accent, "Well, Mr. Beach, you start out funny, but I get used to it." It was a great compliment, and I got the part.

WOLFgang

During rehearsals for the première of *Don Giovanni*, Mozart had trouble getting the soprano singing the role of Zerlina to shriek believably when the Don makes advances to her. Mozart crept backstage, and when the cue came for the shriek he suddenly grabbed the singer from behind. The result satisfied Mozart. "That," he said, "is how an innocent woman screams when her virtue is in danger."

Un-seam-ly

Beniamino Gigli was appearing in Verdi's *La Forza del Destino*. As Gigli was being borne off on a stretcher, one of the bearers stumbled, and the tenor was dumped on the floor. In his awkward scramble to get back on the stretcher, Gigli's pants ripped up the seat. Luckily, the scene was in a monastery, and Gigli finished the act in a monk's robe.

Tubby or Not Tubby?

The heavyweight soprano with horned helmet and spear is the standard operatic stereotype. When Richard Strauss mentioned that he was working on an opera, *Die Frau ohne Schatten* (The Woman Without a Shadow), a critic asked, "Where is he going to find a German prima donna who can impersonate a woman without a shadow?"

Eileen Farrell, a singer of notable gifts and girth, once showed that her sense of humor was the size of her talent. She arrived at an opera rehearsal and said, "They're shipping my costume in a boxcar."

67

They All Passed Out

When Anna Moffo gave her first performance as Gilda in Verdi's *Rigoletto* at London's Covent Garden, several members of the audience were clearly seeing the opera for the first time. Had they studied the synopsis in the program, a lot of confusion could have been avoided. Miss Moffo had just concluded her first duet in Act I when the pressure of the evening overcame her, and she fainted, kerplop, into the arms of Rigoletto. The stage manager discreetly rang down the curtain. At this point, a number of people apparently thought it was the first intermission and headed for the bars.

Ding-Dong

In *La Traviata*, there's a moment at which Violetta uses a little bell to ring for her maid. The prop department goofed during one production, and the bell wasn't there when Violetta needed it. With no time to lose, the singer did a pantomime of a little bell, and anxiously, consumptively, she said, "Tinkle-tinkle?"

Screaming Mimi

In the first act of Puccini's *La Bohème*, Rodolfo is pretending to search for Mimi's lost key. He gropes about in the dark, touches Mimi's cold little hand, and sings "Che gelida manina" (How cold your little hand is). Enrico Caruso was a notorious practical joker. Once, just as he sang the opening words, he produced a hot potato from his pocket and pressed it firmly into her cold little hand. "...se la lasci riscaldar" (...let me warm it here in mine).

In Act Four, as Mimi lies dying of consumption, Musetta gives her an elegant fur muff to warm her hands. Mimi joyfully plunges them into the muff and sighs happily. During a production of this splendid tear-jerker, Frederick Jägel, another trickster, contrived to hide an object in the muff. Mimi sighed with pleasure as she slid her hands into the furry depths, and found herself grasping a warm Polish sausage.

Preobrazhenskoye

It wasn't until the middle of the 17th century that the first opera production was seen in Russia. Czar Alexis imported a company from Germany to present *The Acts of Artaxerxes* to celebrate the birth of the new Czarevich, who grew up to become Peter the Great. Alexis even had a theater built for the occasion at his summer palace at Preobrazhenskoye. It was something of a waste as far as Peter was concerned, because he never developed any interest in music. But, at least, opera had finally come to Russia.

Twain on Wagner

Wagner is pretty strong stuff for some people. Mark Twain was one of those who'd much rather be elsewhere when the leitmotifs begin flowing. His own words: "There isn't often anything in a Wagner opera that one could call by such a violent name as acting. As a rule, all you would see would be a couple of people, one of them standing still, and the other catching flies."

¡Olé!

Many years ago, in Madrid, a production of Wagner's *Götterdämmerung* was blighted by a singer whose performance as the super-duper hero Siegfried was really verschtunken. The singer did so badly that when the treacherous Hagen laid Siegfried low with a spear thrust, the audience burst into a spontaneous ovation.

Cat Scratches

Baudelaire said this: "I love Wagner . . . but the music I prefer is that of a cat hung up by the tail outside a window, and trying to stick to the glass with its claws. There is an odd grating on the glass which I find at the same time strange, irritating, and singularly harmonious."

"An opera house is an institution differing from other lunatic asylums only in the fact that its inmates have avoided certification."
—Ernest Newman

"Opera is when a guy gets stabbed in the back and instead of bleeding he sings."

—Ed Gardner

71

Man:
"I gotta horse named Opera."
Another Man:
"Why did you name your horse Opera?"
Man:
"Because he runs very Faust."

One of the earliest performances of Gounod's *Faust* was plagued with technical flaws. After the overture, only the left side of the curtain went up, leaving half the stage covered. Faust looked into his crystal ball, seeking answers to eternal questions. "rien, je ne vois rien!" (Nothing! I see nothing). A wag in the audience shouted, "Moi non plus!" (Me neither!) Then, when Mephistopheles was supposed to appear in a puff of smoke, the trapdoor jammed, and the basso got a nasty bump on the head. He scrambled onto the stage like a drunken sewer worker from a manhole.

"Opera is an exotic and irrational entertainment."

— Dr. Samuel Johnson

Other than that...

Few composers have ever received more critical invective than Richard Wagner. One writer, after hearing a performance of *Die Meistersinger* in the 1860s threw restraint to the winds: "Of all the clumsy, lumbering, boggling, baboon-blooded stuff I ever saw on a human stage, of all the affected, sapless, soul-less, beginningless, endless, topless, bottomless, topsy-turviest doggerel of sound I ever endured the deadliness of, that eternity of nothing was the deadliest."

Juan, Two, Three, Four...

In Mozart's *Don Giovanni*, Leporello sings a famous aria in which he recites the catalogue of the Don's amorous conquests. The roster includes 640 in Italy, 231 in Germany, an even 100 in France, and in Turkey 91. But in Spain, no fewer than 1,003! That comes to 2,065 presumably satisfied customers. It makes you wonder what Don Giovanni did in his spare time.

> In opera, "anything that is too stupid to be spoken is sung."
>
> —Voltaire

Carmen-taries

If Don José had popped the question and gotten a "Yes!" his wife would have become Carmen Lizzarrabengoa. In Prosper Merimée's original story, the soldier who goes bananas and AWOL over the sultry heroine is named Don José Lizzarrabengoa de Navarre. Carmen *did* have a husband, though. In Merimée's story he gets killed by Don José, making Carmen the Widow Garcia.

✶

If you want to amaze your friends with further operatic trivia, tell them there was no toreador in that original story, no Escamillo. It was a picador, and his name was Lucas.

✶

Many people mistakenly pronounce the title of Carmen's big aria with a little squiggle, or tilde, over the "n": "Habañera." It's really just "Habanera," meaning "In the style of Havana, Cuba." Bizet stole it, by the way . . . found a tune called "El Areglito," by a Spaniard named Yradier, and just swiped it for his opera.

✶

At the New York City Opera, Joseph Rosenstock was conducting a production of *Carmen*. David Poleri, the tenor singing Don José, was decidedly unfond of Rosenstock's handling of the tempi and dynamics. At one point, Poleri lost all restraint and left the stage, saying, "Finish the opera yourself!"

I once saw a production of *Carmen* with a six-foot tall mezzo in the title role. The tenor was a little runt, and he had to reach way up to stab her in the middle. She went down like a pine tree.

74

Miscellaneous

Tuneful Plumbing

The largest musical instrument ever made, and possibly the loudest, is the pipe organ at the Atlantic City Auditorium in New Jersey. The console of this enormous mass of tuneful plumbing has seven manuals. There's even a second console with five manuals, a portable model. 1,477 stops control 33,112 pipes, and the blowers develop 365 horsepower. At full volume, the ophicleide stop is more than six times louder than a steam-locomotive whistle, enough to leave the average rock band standing respectful, with hat in hand.

Lugubrious

Voltaire has been widely quoted . . . but his views of matters musical haven't been so well remembered. The same man who said, "I may not agree with what you say, but I shall defend, to the death, your right to say it," also said, "The most High has a decided taste for vocal music, provided it be lugubrious and gloomy enough."

Allons, Enfants

Rouget de Lisle composed "La Marseillaise," right? Well, not exactly. What he *did* compose was a "Battle-Song for the Army of the Rhine." He was a captain in the French garrison at Strasbourg, and the mayor of the town asked him to write a marching song. That was in April of 1792. Four months later, on August 10, some soldiers from Marseilles sang the song as they advanced on the Tuilleries. That's how the song got its historic name. Rouget de Lisle wasn't even a revolutionary. He was a royalist, and he darn-near got his head chopped off.

Batter Up!

The Great American Pastime, as everyone knows, is baseball. Or is it? In 1968, at the opening of the San Francisco Symphony season, Joseph Krips led the orchestra in "The Star-Spangled Banner" to begin the concert. At the final brave note, a voice from the balcony shouted, "Play ball!"

C

The time-signature "C" does *not* indicate "common" time. In ancient music, "perfect" time had three beats per measure, corresponding with the Trinity. The symbol for perfect time was a circle. Music in four beats was considered "imperfect," and its symbol was an incomplete circle: C. So, when you see a C, count four and start playing.

Flash

At the old Metropolitan Opera House in New York, the stage wiring was a building inspector's nightmare, a mess of tangled wires and cobbled fixtures. It was also the bane of one silver flute.

Frederick Wilkins was a flutist in the Met's orchestra. During a performance, with a very long rest in the flute part, Wilkins placed his instrument on the edge of the stage apron. There was a flash, and the flute melted.

Suicide

Jeremiah Clark was the organist at St. Paul's Cathedral very early in the 18th century. He fell in love with a noblewoman of the parish, but his affections were not returned. The despairing Clark decided that suicide was the only relief for his pain. But how? Hanging? Drowning? He flipped a coin. It landed on clay soil, remaining on its edge. He went home and shot himself. It worked.

"Quiet, you lousy amateurs!"

Ben Hecht leased a Hollywood mansion during the film capital's "golden era." With a group of friends, he formed the Ben Hecht Symphonietta. The players included Charles MacArthur, Charlie Lederer, George Antheil, and Harpo Marx.

During a rehearsal in an upstairs room, the door flew open and a voice shouted, "Quiet, you lousy amateurs!" It was Groucho Marx, who was miffed at being excluded from the ensemble. He played the mandolin, which the members of the Symphonietta considered undignified. The rehearsal continued, ignoring the interruption.

A few moments later, the whole house was engulfed in huge musical sounds. Groucho had hired the entire Los Angeles Philharmonic and quietly brought the orchestra into the house.

The amazed Symphoniettans came down to the strains of Wagner's *Tannhäuser* Overture as Groucho waved his arms like a self-satisfied pterodactyl.

Remote Broadcast

The first remote broadcast wasn't done by radio but by long-distance telephone. In 1877, at Steinway Hall in New York, an audience heard a performance from Philadelphia of Elisha Gray's "Transmission of Music by Telegraph," featuring "Home, Sweet Home," "The Last Rose of Summer," and "Yankee Doodle."

Die schöne grüne Donau

"The Blue Danube" is a beautiful waltz but an inaccurate title. A Viennese observer kept tabs on the Danube for a full year. On 255 days the river was green, on 60 it was gray, there were 40 yellow days, and on 10 days the Danube was brown. That comes to 365 days . . . and the Danube was never once blue. If Strauss had looked, he might have written "The Brown Danube."

Long Handle

In the late 1700s and early 1800s, there was a vogue in Europe for "battle music" . . . pieces composed to memorialize and celebrate the great battles and skirmishes that kept happening. One such composition bears a title almost longer than the piece: "The Battle of Würzburg on the 3rd of September, 1796, Between the Royal Imperial Army Under the Command of His Imperial Highness the Archduke Karl of Austria, Imperial Field Marshal, and the Enemy French Troops Under the Command of General Jourdan, by Mr. Johann Wanhal."

80

O.K.; We Didn't Forget It

When Walter Slezak wrote his autobiography, he borrowed a line from his father as the title. Leo Slezak was rehearsing for a presentation of *Lohengrin*. The stage crew jumped their cue and pulled the swan-boat offstage before Slezak could embark. He turned and got off the line which Walter was to use: "What time does the next swan leave?"

81

You Can't Play That

Theobald Boehm was a virtuoso flutist and an inventor. In 1835, he introduced a great improvement in flute design. The Boehm flute was considerably easier to play than previous flutes, and its tone was far superior. Boehm wanted Rossini to know of his invention. One day, he visited the composer and stationed himself in a room next to one in which Rossini was shaving. He began playing some highly complicated flute passages. In a few moments, Rossini came in with lather on his face: "You cannot play that!" Boehm smiled, "But I am playing it." "I don't care if you are...it is utterly impossible!"

Bring a Friend

A Viennese music critic died without leaving enough money to pay for a funeral and burial. His friends went to a well-known composer and asked him to contribute. "What's my share?" he asked. "Thirty kronen, Maestro." The composer said, "Here's sixty kronen. Bury two critics."

Sure!

Most likely this story never really happened, but it's still a good story. A symphony orchestra was playing an outdoor concert in Central Park. One of the second violinists was bowing away when a bird flew by and scored a direct hit. The musician gave a resigned shrug and said, "For other people, you sing."

Oomp-pah

I was the principal sousaphone player in the Lake Oswego Grammar School band. I was also the only sousaphone player in that spendid ensemble. As a seventh grader, I oomped and pahed my part in "Pomp and Circumstance" while the eighth grade graduation exercises unfolded before proud parents and faculty. As the solemn academic procession made its step-and-pause entrance, I was seized with an onslaught of hiccups. Sousaphones amplify hiccups. And, to this day, Mrs. Inkster, the music teacher, believes I was an assassin hired by the enemy to make a shambles of that graduation.

Here's the Champ

Here's one of the all-time chestnuts. It's been told of the Goldman Band in Central Park, the Philadelphia Orchestra in Fairmont Park, and numberless others: An outdoor concert featured Beethoven's third *Leonore* Overture. It calls for a fanfare on an offstage trumpet. When the cue came for the fanfare, nothing happened. Backstage, the trumpeter was wrestling with a policeman who insisted, "You can't blow that thing here! There's a concert going on!"

83

Oh shay, can you shee . . . ?

I have a theory that Francis Scott Key was drunk when he wrote "The Star-Spangled Banner." "Libelous!" you say? Read on.

Key spent that night of September 13 and 14, 1814, on the deck of a ship, watching the battle of Fort McHenry. It stands to reason that a fellow'd welcome a few belts at such a time, what with the chilly air and the anxiety and all.

Now, there was a club in those days, The Anacreontic Society, dedicated to good music and good booze. The club was founded in England, but it's quite possible that Key was a member of the American branch. The official song of The Anacreontic Society was a lusty, rollicking anthem in praise of revelry, "To Anacreon In Heav'n."

By the early light of that historic dawn, Key saw that the flag of his country was still waving over the fort. "We beat 'em! Yahoo!" Blinking bleary eyes, he fished an envelope from his pocket and sketched several verses destined to stir the hearts of Americans and stretch their vocal cords with the rockets' red glare.

Here are the words of the first verse of "To Anacreon In Heav'n":

> To Anacreon in Heav'n, where he sat in full
>   glee,
> A few sons of harmony sent a petition
> That he their inspirer and leader should be;
> When this answer arrived from the jolly old
>   Grecian:
>   Voice, fiddle and flute,
>   No longer be mute!
> I'll lend ye my name, and inspire ye to boot.
> And, besides, I'll instruct ye, like me, to
>   entwine
> The myrtle of Venus with Bacchus' vine!

If that envelope could be found, I bet the first verse would begin: "Oh shay, can you shee . . . ?"

"Nothing is capable of being well set to music that is not nonsense."

—Joseph Addison

Second Fiddle

A wealthy man in Cleveland was proud of his son's violin playing. When the boy was old enough, he was enrolled in a conservatory, and his father promised to endow the school with a fat check. But a few weeks later, the deal was off. There was an evening of chamber music in which the young man played second violin. His father was incensed. "I didn't send him here to study second anything!" The conservatory never got the fat check.

Papal Opera

In 1639, two Italian composers, Virgilio Mazzocchi and Marco Marazzoli, created an opera on a libretto by a man who later went on to higher things. The librettist for *Chi Soffre Speri*, or *He Who Suffers Hopes*, was Guilio Rospigliosi, a Cardinal of the R.C.C. who, in 1667, became Pope Clement the 9th.

Schieferdecker

When Diederich Buxtehude was appointed organist at St. Mary's Church in Lübeck, it was on condition that he marry the daughter of Tunder, his predecessor. Buxtehude accepted this Tunderbolt and had a happy career at the console. When he retired, he tried to continue the tradition by insisting that his successor take his daughter, Anna Margreta, to wife. Handel and Mattheson wanted the job, but not that much, and they said, "Danke, nein." So did Johann Sebastian Bach, who admired Buxtehude; but one look at Anna Margreta was enough. Bach said, "Auf wiedersehen." What Anna Margreta Buxtehude said is not recorded. It took three years to find a man who could play both the organ and the role of husband. At last, wedded bliss was hers, and the guests threw rice at Anna Margreta Buxtehude-Schieferdecker.

"Swans sing before they die. 'Twere no bad thing
Should certain persons die before they sing."
—Samuel Taylor Coleridge

Friend to Casanova

When Lorenzo da Ponte wasn't busy writing a libretto for one of Mozart's operas, he appears to have been dallying with married women or dodging their outraged husbands. In Venice, a number of men went so far as to get a law passed to ban Da Ponte from the city. He moved to Vienna and soon wore out his welcome there in similar fashion. He escaped the Viennese vigilantes and wound up in New York, teaching Italian at Columbia College and running a grocery store.

Well-Tempered

"The Well-Tempered Clavier" . . . ever wonder where it got that name? Well, way back when, musical instruments were tuned according to a simple and precise mathematical system. And people played wonderfully in tune. The trouble was that, under the old system of so-called "just" tuning," you could only play in one or two keys without retuning your instrument or getting a different one already tuned in the other key. So along came the tempered scale, a system of adjusting the perfect, mathematical ratios of "just" tuning so that you could change keys without a lot of hassle. We learned how to fudge a bit here and a bit there, and now we can play out of tune equally well in all keys. Now, on your piano, A-sharp and B-flat are the same note. If they weren't, as in the old way of tuning, you'd have to have a whole houseful of pianos in order to be able to play in any old key. So be happy. The tempered scale has saved you a bundle and a lot of room.

Was ist das?

The first time Richard Wagner heard the sound of a saxophone, his impression was definitely negative. When asked what he thought of the instrument, he then and there coined a word thirty letters long to describe the impression it gave him. Wagner said, "It sounds like somebody saying, 'Reckankreuzungsklankewerkzeuge'!"

This qualifies as something of an in-joke, I suppose. A musician once invited a colleague to meet him for lunch. The invitation said, "The pleasure of your company is requested for luncheon, key of G." A layman would have been confused by this, but not a musician. He read it correctly and met his friend at one — sharp.

"An interval is the distance from one piano to the next."
—From a student's essay

"Music helps not the toothache."
—George Herbert

"Flute, n. A variously perforated hollow stick intended for the punishment of sin, the minister of retribution being commonly a young man with straw-colored eyes and lean hair."
—Ambrose Bierce

"Bach was the master of the fudge, also the feud."
—From a student's essay

"I played over the music of that scoundrel Brahms. What a giftless bastard!"
—Tchaikowsky

"The typical Wagnerian soprano looks like an ox, she moves like a cart-horse, she stands like a haystack."
—Ernest Newman

"Wagner was born in the year 1813, supposedly on his birthday."
—From a student's essay

"Wagner has beautiful moments but awful quarter hours."
—Rossini

"Piano, n. A parlor utensil for subduing the impenitent visitor. It is operated by depressing the keys of the machine and the spirits of the audience."
—Ambrose Bierce

''The best cello players have bow legs.''
— From a student's essay

''Coloratura: compulsive cough.''
—Renato Capecchi

''Beethoven wrote three symphonies:
the First, the Fifth and the Ninth.''
— From a student's essay

''Syncopation is emphasis on a note that is not
in the piece.''
—From a student's essay

90

"I never use a score when conducting my orchestra. Does a lion tamer enter a cage with a book on how to tame a lion?"
—Dimitri Mitropolous*

*See also "You Can Tell the Players Without a Score" on page 9.

91

"Singer: vocal biped, male or female, common throughout the world. Lover of myths and a convinced victim. Generally indigestible; only brain may be savored, when available."

—Renato Capecchi

"A vile beastly rottenheaded foolbegotten brazenthroated pernicious piggish screaming, tearing, roaring, perplexing, splitmecrackle, crashmecriggle insane ass of a woman is practising howling below-stairs with a brute of a singingmaster so horribly that my head is nearly off."

—Edward Lear

"I only know two tunes. One of them is 'Yankee Doodle,' and the other one isn't."

—U. S. Grant

[to an erring orchestra] "After I die, I shall return to earth as the doorkeeper of a bordello and I won't let a one of you in."

—Arturo Toscanini

"Clarionet, n. An instrument of torture operated by a person with cotton in his ears. There are two instruments that are worse than a clarionet—two clarionets."

—Ambrose Bierce

Q: When Verdi's *Aïda* was first performed at the Metropolitan Opera on November 12, 1886, who had trouble remembering the Italian words?
A: Nobody. The performance was done in German.

93

"Rimsky-Korsakov—what a name! It suggests fierce whiskers stained with vodka!"
—*Musical Courier*

"Fiddle, n. An instrument to tickle human ears by friction of a horse's tail on the entrails of a cat."
—Ambrose Bierce

"If you think you've hit a false note, sing loud. When in doubt, sing loud."
—Robert Merrill

"Sibelius is a nationalist. He is Polish, through and through."
—From a student's essay

"In my opinion, the desire to push works of art beyond the realm of art means simply to drive them into the realm of folly. Richard Strauss is in the process of showing us the road."
—Camille Saint-Saëns

"To listen is an effort, and just to hear is no merit. A duck hears also."
—Igor Stravinsky

"There are three degrees of comparison: stupido, stupidissimo, and tenore."
—Pietro Mascagni

[on women in the orchestra] "A pretty one will distract the other musicians, and an ugly one will distract me."
—Sir Thomas Beecham

Rats

People who are not fond of so-called modern music will smile at this one. In the name of science, a team of researchers at the University of Texas once rigged loudspeakers in the cages of

two groups of rats. Mozart was played to one group . . . and Schoenberg was played to the other. The Mozartified rats got along fine . . . but the Schoenbergees went bonkers.

Q. A certain singer had the distinction of performing at the funerals of Haydn in 1809, Beethoven in 1827, and Chopin in 1849. For a whole flock of points, name that singer.
A. Luigi Lablache. Lablache was a celebrated basso, a veritable giant of a man. (See "Tall Story," p. 51.) He also once taught singing to Queen Victoria.

Q. At all three of those funerals of Haydn, Beethoven, and Chopin, the same musical work was performed. Name that tune!
A. Mozart's *Requiem*. At the Haydn obsequies, Lablache was a boy contralto. At the others, he sang the bass solos.

Q. The opening chorus of Gilbert and Sullivan's *Mikado* begins with the words, "Miya Sama." What do they mean?

A. "Miya is a princely title. "Sama" is honorific, usually abbreviated to San. Miya Sama would thus be Honorable Prince. In Japan, one would address an assembly of people such as a board of directors, a gaggle of geishas, or the standees in line to buy this book as Miya Sama! (Honorable Everybody!)

Q. P. T. Barnum was the impresario for Jenny Lind's tour of the United States in 1850. How much money did the Swedish Nightingale realize from her American appearances?
A. $176,675.09.

Q. Just before Custer led his troops out of Fort Lincoln, heading for the Little Bighorn, the band played the Seventh Cavalry's battle tune. Can you name that massacral overture?
A. "Garry Owen."

Q. Most national anthems tend either to extol a monarch, emperor, pasha, or poobah, or to commemorate some bloody but successful encounter. The national anthems of Bahrain and Qatar, however, neither extol nor commemorate anything. Explain.
A. Neither of those national tunes has any words at all.

Q. If you were to set your metronome at 132, sit at the piano, and play Czerny's "Etude #740" for one hour, at four notes to the tick, how many notes would tinkle from your talented fingers in that time?
A. 31,680.

Q. Can you name the oldest waltz in captivity?
A. "Ach du lieber Augustin," composed in 1770.

Q. What was Enrico Caruso's recipe for a gargle to get his throat ready for singing?
A. After sniffing a pinch of Swedish snuff to clear his nostrils, Caruso gargled lukewarm salt water, followed by a sip of diluted whiskey.

Q. Beethoven composed nine symphonies, all of which are still played today. Johann Melchior Molter composed *169* symphonies. How many of Molter's works are still in the repertoire?
A. Do I really have to tell you?

Q. If Jacques Offenbach were alive today, how much money would the U.S. government owe him?
A. A bundle! Offenbach's comic opera *Genèvieve de Brabant* contains a rousing martial tune, "Couplets des Hommes de l'Armée." That tune is the melody of the Marine's Hymn, "The Halls of Montezuma."

Q. What is the world's largest brass instrument?

A. It's a tuba, built for John Philip Sousa's band. The monster contained 39 feet of tubing from oomp to pah, and it measured 90 inches from bell to butt.

Q. Robert Schumann suffered from a terrible melancholia. He also had the nagging problem of a particular musical note constantly sounding in his head ... said it gave him the fidgets. What was that note?

A. A-440. A slightly sharp or flat A drove him bonkers.

Q. If a body meet a body, comin' through the rye, they both are likely to have wet feet. How come?

A. They're crossing a river. The song refers to the fording of the River Rye. By custom, a lassie crossing the Rye would be hailed and asked to pay a toll of one kiss. Shall we gather by the river?

No Erik

As a student, I visited the Paris Opéra and had a guided tour of that gingerbread palace. It was fascinating. I especially remember discovering, five levels below the stage, the inspiration for *The Phantom of the Opera*. If you know the story, you remember that the Phantom meets his doom when his underground hideaway is flooded. Well, way down under the main stage, there's a metal grillwork covering a hole in the floor. By the beam of a flashlight, I saw an underground lagoon. I listened closely for a long moment, but if Lon Chaney or Claude Rains was down there, he never said a word.

Room for Improvement

King George III took violin lessons from a teacher named Salomon, who told his nibs, "Fiddlers, your Majesty, may be divided into three classes. To the first belong those who cannot play at all; to the second those who play badly; and to the third those who play well. You, sire, have already achieved the second class."

"Noise, n. A stench in the ear. Undomesticated music. The chief product and authenticating sign of civilization."

—Ambrose Bierce

"Hell is full of musical amateurs; music is the brandy of the damned."

—George Bernard Shaw

"Nobody really sings in an opera—they just make loud noises."

—Amelita Galli-Curci

"Contralto is a low sort of music that only ladies sing."

—From a student's essay

"The correct way to find the key to a piece of music is with a pitch-fork."

— From a student's essay

Going to the Dogs

During a Saturday matinee of *Swan Lake* in Portland, Oregon, Alexandra Danilova was dancing the lead. The danseuse and her audience began to notice strange sounds, like the distant barking of dogs. That's what it was. In the basement of the Civic Auditorium, the Multnomah Kennel Club was having a dog show. Danilova no doubt wondered if, during one of her "Black Swan" solos, a pack of dogs would storm onto the set and finish her off.

A few years ago, Aaron Copland, the dean of American composers, remarked: "If a literary man puts together two words about music, one of them will be wrong." Possibly he was hoping to scare writers away from the field of music. I don't scare that easy. In an era that has seen the coining of the term "credibility," I figure a 50/50 chance of being right is a damn good bet.

Many literary figures have put together words about music. In the "Don Juan in Hell" portion of *Man and Superman*, George Bernard Shaw fired off a great line. Shaw, of course, was also a prominent music critic. In the play, the Devil bristles at a slighting reference to "...a hysterical woman, fawning over a fiddler." The Don replies, "Hell is full of musical amateurs. Music is the brandy of the damned. May not one lost soul be permitted to abstain?"

In the middle of the 17th century, the prolific writer Anon, who must have heard some base, vile music (on a bass viol?), wrote this couplet:

Music is but a fart that's sent
From the guts of an instrument.

And early in the last century, a rather crusty fellow named William Cobbett sounded a warning to anyone who might feel tempted to strum, beat, bow, blow, finger, or vocalize: "A great fondness for music is a mark of great weakness, great vacuity of mind; not of hardness of heart; not of vice; not of downright folly; but of a want of capacity, or inclination, for sober thought."

Yes, but where does that leave Bach, Beethoven, Brahms, Webern, Walton, and Welk? Come to think of it, though, just because you make your living with music, you aren't necessarily fond of it. I've heard a good many people playing or singing as if they hated it. I suspect, though, that old Cobbett was simply tasting the sour grapes of a lifelong inability to carry a tune.

Musicians often have only themselves to blame for the attacks made on them. Everybody knows, for instance, that all jazz musicians and rock stars are dope fiends, and opera singers are gourmandizers. Some of the crankiest and most outrageous characters in history are musicians. Take Wagner...please. (By the way, did you know that his first name wasn't Richard? It was Wilhelm. Wilhelm Richard Wagner.)

It's a good thing for Wagner's place in the musical pantheon that he composed a number of important operas. Without those masterpieces to give him some respectability, he'd have gone into the books as a self-indulgent, licentious, overbearing, and thoroughly kinky person.

But posterity tends to overlook and forgive almost anything, so long as you leave behind a gigantic, awe-inspiring, and monumental bunch of operas, symphonies, paintings, books, or whatnot. Think it over.

Nietzsche admired Wagner for many years ... thought he was a genius and a fine man. But then, something happened, and talk about picky! Nietzsche cut loose with both barrels: "Is Wagner human at all? Is he not rather a disease? He contaminates everything he touches—he has made music sick. I postulate this viewpoint: Wagner's art is diseased."

Aw hell, Fred, nobody's perfect. Besides, where I come from, folks don't often postulate viewpoints. Mostly, they just say, claim, or allow-as-how. Nietzsche'd have had few friends in Lake Oswego, Oregon. I've seen people standing three and four deep to see Wagner's operas. Who, I ask you, has seen that kind of crowd standing at the 193 shelves of the library?

Throughout history, musicians have had terrible problems with their social and economic status. Most of the great composers of the past were paid little or nothing for the work. And they were commonly treated like the lowest menials. Singers and instrumentalists rarely did any better. The guilds and labor unions of today were formed largely to combat just such conditions. The Musicians' Union has done a lot of good ... but occasionally, well ...

When Victor Borge did his famous one-man show on Broadway, he was obliged to hire an orchestra, though none was needed for his solo act. A New York producer, Arthur Cantor, once had a similar problem. When the union demanded that he engage eight musicians he didn't need, he went into action.

Cantor informed the union that he would comply, and asked for two string quartets, one all-male and one all-female. When the players arrived at the theater in Philadelphia for the first rehearsals, they were directed to the men's and women's restrooms, where chairs and music stands were set up. There wasn't anything in the rules about where the musicians must play. The playgoers were treated to Bach's Brandenburg Concerti as they pondered the message of the play. (You probably thought I was going to get in a line about Cantor being flushed with pride. Hah!)

Since that memorable occasion, the rules have been changed. Nowadays, if you're stuck with unneeded players, you've got to stick them in the orchestra pit or in one of the boxes.

Time was, when you wanted a little music you made it yourself or you went without. There, in your cave, mud hut, hogan, lean-to, or split-level cliff-dwelling, you beat on your fallen enemy or stomped on the floor, or you growled love's old, sweet growl, and your savage breast was soothed.

Then people got more organized and civilized. They invented the wheel, fought wars, hired musicians. It wasn't long before music became as common as cordwood, and musicians were everywhere. To cope with this glut, more complicated instruments were invented, and more difficult music was composed. Heads of state and wealthy people had pipe-organs installed, and they hired musicians to fill the house with music at the wave of a lace hanky.

When the industrial revolution came along, music began to burgeon. Theaters, concert halls, opera houses sprang up. Then, radio, and phonograph records, and television, and, God help us, Muzak! Music was everywhere! We were inundated with it. In elevators, lavatories, waiting rooms, surgeries, anywhere there was a captive audience, there was music. There was no escape!

Finally, the atmosphere of the earth became so overloaded with music that crops failed, schools closed because nobody could hear for the din, and earplug stocks soared. Fortunately, the governments of the world managed to agree that something had to be done to check the universal hullabaloo. By mutual consent, all forms of music were prohibited for one year to permit the world to quiet down. A papal encyclical, "Tacet

Tutti!" was whispered into the Congressional Record.

A bill, sponsored jointly by ASCAP and The Sierra Club, was passed unanimously by both Houses and the General Assembly to permit a limited amount of music on a per-acre basis. From now on, before you sing even "Happy Birthday," you'll have to file an Environmental Impact Report.

108

"A true music lover is one who,
on hearing a soprano singing in a bathtub,
puts his ear to the keyhole."

— Anon

109

ACKNOWLEDGMENTS

Some of the stories in this book came to me by word of mouth. (Curious term, "word of mouth." Anybody ever gotten a story by word of elbow?) Others were found in the following publications:

Antheil, George. *Bad Boy of Music.* Doubleday, Doran & Company, Inc.

Bloomfield, Arthur. *Fifty Years of the San Francisco Opera.* San Francisco Book Co.

Borge, Victor. *My Favorite Intermissions.* Doubleday and Company, Inc.

Crowest, Frederick J. *Musicians' Wit, Humor & Anecdote.* The Walter Scott Publishing Co., Ltd. Republished by Gryphon Books.

Dickson, Harry Ellis. *Gentlemen, More Dolce Please!* Beacon Press

Ewen, David. *Dictators of the Baton.* Ziff-Davis Publishing Company

Fink, Henry T. *Musical Laughs.* Funk & Wagnalls Company.

Grove's Dictionary of Music and Musicians. St. Martin's Press.

Kaufmann, Helen L. *Anecdotes of Music and Musicians.* Grosset & Dunlap.

Levant, Oscar. *A Smattering of Ignorance.* Doubleday, Doran & Co., Inc.

Morgenstern, Sam, Editor. *Composers on Music.* Pantheon Books.

Reid, Charles. *Thomas Beecham.* Readers Union-Victor Gollancz, Ltd.

Schonberg, Harold C. *The Great Conductors.* Simon & Schuster.

Slonimsky, Nicolas. *A Thing or Two About Music.* Allen, Towne & Heath, Inc. Reprinted by Greenwood Press.

Slonimsky, Nicolas. *Lexicon of Musical Invective.* Coleman-Ross Company, Inc. Washington Paperback.

Sonneck, Oscar. *Report on the Star-Spangled Banner, Hail Columbia, America and Yankee Doodle.* Dover Publications.

Taylor, Deems. *Of Men and Music.* Simon & Schuster.

111